WOLF DAYS IN PENNSYLVANIA

METALMARK BOOKS

⅛ Natural Size   BLACK WOLF (*Canis Lycaon*)   (Frontispiece)

To C. W. DICKINSON
Greatest Living Pennsylvania Wolf Hunter
These Pages Are Respectfully Dedicated

INDEX

———

Wolf Days in Pennsylvania

AN OLD IRISH SHEEP-FOLD
(Design by Miss Katharine H. McCormick)

By HENRY W. SHOEMAKER

President of Altoona Tribune
Altoona, Penna.

PROFUSELY ILLUSTRATED

Published by THE TRIBUNE PRESS
1 9 1 4

I. PREFACE.

THAT a new book treating on the much-discussed wolf can be written at all, the animal must be described from an entirely different point of view, else it would be superfluous. Happily the author feels that there is a side, an important one, to the wolfish character, which has been overlooked or perverted. It is a side decidedly favorable to the animal, to its inherent right to live, to be protected by mankind. The wolf of Pennsylvania accomplished much more good than harm. At the time when the Indians ranged the Continent and Nature's balance was perfect, the wolf played an important role. It preyed upon the weak and sickly animals and birds, preventing the perpetuation of imperfect types and the spread of pestilences. It kept up a high standard of excellence among all lesser creatures, was the great preserver of type and perfection. In addition it devoured bugs, insects, grubs and worms of an injur-

DAVID A. ZIMMERMAN AND WIFE
Mr. Zimmerman was the great Hunter who drove the Wolves out of Sugar Valley

ious nature. When the white man appeared on the scene and began killing all living things indiscriminately, the food supply of the wolves was affected. The wolfish diet required meat, and this at times became unobtainable. Crazed with hunger the wolves attacked calves, pigs and sheep, which slow of motion and easily captured, occupied the same relative position to them as had the formerly abundant weak and imperfect deer, grouse, rabbits and quail. Just as some otherwise harmless men commit murder when crazed by lack of food, the wolves played havoc in farm yards that otherwise they would have left unmolested. As the result, bounties were put on their heads, they were hunted unmercifully. The wolves were also useful forest scavengers, cleaning up the neighborhoods of camps and hunters' shambles. No person stopped to reason if the wolves had a useful purpose in the world—man deliberately acted as if the Wise Maker had erred in creating such animals. All living things have a *purpose;* it would be a loss to the world if even the common house flies were completely exterminated. It is an over-production of any one species of thing that carries the germ of trouble. Consequently the panther, the sworn enemy of the wolf, kept that species down to proper numbers; the Indian, sworn foe of the panther, kept the "Pennsylvania Lion" within bounds—but there was no warfare of extermination until the white man came. Most of the early hunters came of peasant stock, unused to carrying firearms in the old country, and with deeply rooted feelings against private parks which preserved

10

game. Once loosed in a new continent, given arms and freedom, they set out to slaughter everything in sight. They wanted excuses for wholesale killing; the wolves' thefts of calves, pigs and sheep gave it to them. If they had killed less of the wolves' food supply no farm stock would have been taken. In Africa the same horrible story is being re-enacted. The zebras break down wire fences, they must go; the rhinosceroses frighten the oxen, they must go; the hippos are dangerous to navigation, they must go; the elephants trample the grain fields; they must go; the giraffes knock down the telegraph wires, they must go; the lions are bloodthirsty, they must go, and so on, every animal is marked for extermination by the rapacious settlers. And only too often the powers that be sitting in London, Paris or Berlin acquiesce unwittingly to the slaughter, and "abrogate the game law." The early settlers of America were unhampered by game laws, their blood lust knew no bounds. The wolves were starved into criminal acts, and then punished for it. Now after the wolves are gone a more discriminating generation looks over the scene dispassionately and notes that nothing has been gained by their extirpation. In Scotland when wolves abounded no one ever heard of "grouse" disease or "rabbit" disease; the ibex and chamois in Switzerland deteriorated after the wolves disappeared. The ibex exists in Italy where there are wolves, and as long as there are wolves there will be ibexes. In Africa buffaloes and certain antelopes diminish as the lions are killed off. The rinder-

11

pest rages in regions where there are no longer any lions, leopards or cheetahs. In Pennsylvania the harm done by the destruction of wolves has been appalling. First of all the increase in insect pests. These were practically unknown when panthers, wolves and foxes were prevalent. Secondly, the race of deer has deteriorated. the larger varieties *Odocoileus Americanus Borealis Miller* is completely extinct. The race of deer is only kept up by frequent introductions of specimens from Western States *where there are wolves*. The grouse are getting scarcer, despite "man-made" game laws; disease ravages them every few seasons. The big hares are gone, rabbits not what they were, the quail are frail; sickly specimens breed now; formerly the wolves prevented that.

Any reader detecting inaccuracies in this book will be conferring a great favor by communicating with the author so as to prevent their repetition in a second edition.

II. THE LAST WOLF—WHO GETS THE CREDIT?

FROM the mass of data and the number of claimants it is indeed difficult to award the palm for the slayer of the last wolf in Pennsylvania. In the first place, in order to eliminate a few of the strivers for the coveted title, slayers of wolves which have wandered in from other states must be counted out. This will rule out the celebrated "Beaver Dam Wolf" which was killed in Portage Township, near the borders of Blair and Cambria Counties, by Messrs. Jacob Royer and Samuel Long, farmers of Turkey Valley, in May, 1907. This animal, which weighed, according to a correspondent in the Altoona Tribune, nearly eighty-five pounds and measured almost six feet from tip to tip, was evidently a stray. Its carcass was purchased by Mr. W. E. C. Todd, Assistant Curator of Mammals of the Carnegie Museum in Pittsburg. This will also rule out a huge grey wolf killed by that veteran hunter, "Old John" Aneer in Somerset County, in 1897; four wolves, evidently escaped from some traveling circus, slain in Lackawanna County in 1896; a New York State wolf, also probably escaped from some Zoo, killed by Daniel Rutan in Wayne County in 1887, and a wolf killed by Levi Kissinger in Tioga County in 1885. With these doubtful cases out of the way, the field is clear for an impartial judgment. Seth Iredell Nelson killed two wolves in Clearfield

13

County in February and March, 1892; they were
native brown wolves and the last remnant of the big
pack which for years infested the Divide Region.
Mr. Nelson was in his 83rd year at that time, hence
he can be called the oldest wolf slayer that Pennsylvania has produced. Capt. A. A. Clay, of Ridgway,
Elk County, hunting pal of Col. Roosevelt and an all
around sportsman, states that a native wolf was killed
in Elk County in 1891. No name is given as to who
killed this animal in Rhoads' "Mammals of Pennsylvania and New Jersey." John Razey, a respected
citizen of Sunderlinville, killed a grey wolf in Potter
County in 1890, and received a bounty from the
County Commissioners. The year 1886 was prolific
in kills of native wolves. Dan Treaster, "the Daniel
Boone of the Seven Mountains," killed a magnificent
black wolf that year in Treaster Valley, Mifflin
County, and one George Sizer killed a grey wolf on
Potato Creek, in McKean County. In 1888 Charles
Ives and Theodore Pierce, two boys, killed a lame
grey wolf on Kinzua Creek, McKean County. It had
escaped from one of C. W. Dickinson's traps a few
seasons before. In 1885 Dan Treaster killed two black
wolves in Treaster Valley. In 1884 Emmanuel Dobson
killed the last wolf in Forest County. That year Seth
Iredell Nelson killed five brown wolves in Clearfield
County. Andy Long killed the last wolf in Jefferson
County in 1881. Jake Hamersley killed the last wolf in
Clinton County. In February, 1913, there was a "wolf
scare" in Horse Valley, not far from Chambersburg,

EDWARD H. DICKINSON (1810-1890)
A famous old-time Wolf Hunter of Northern Pennsylvania
(He killed his last Wolf in 1872)

which resulted in the killing of two peculiar looking
dogs, which had evidently adapted themselves to forest
life and running deer. The hide of the male hangs in
the study of the writer of this article. It is a pasty grey
in color. The hide of the bitch, which is in the possession of M. W. Straley, Chambersburg, Pa., is said
to be darker. Doubtless there are records of other
wolves killed in recent years, but up to the time of the
preparation of this treatise they have not come to
light. Certainly wolves were killed in the Seven
Mountains after 1886, in the Clearfield region between 1884 and 1892, and in Potter County within a
year or two of 1890. From the data available it
would seem that Seth Iredell Nelson is the slayer of
the last native wolves, in addition to being the oldest
wolf killer. The Elk County wolf of 1891 is next
in order, but the pity of it is that the hunter's name
is unknown. It is hoped that the party in question
will read this article and come forward. If the person to whom the last bona-fide bounty was paid de-
serves the title, then John Razey, who killed the wolf
in Potter County, is the hero of the exploit, and fit
to rank with MacQueen of Pall-a-Chrocain who killed
the last wolf in Scotland, and Rory Carragh, who in
the Tyrone mountains siew the last Irish wolf. The
personality of John Razey should be better known
and should be given a chance to wear his laurels in
that immortal coterie of Pennsylvania wolf hunters,
which includes such names as Dan Treaster, Seth
Iredell Nelson, Samuel Quinn, of Quinn's Run, who

killed four wolves with a single bullet; C. W. Dickinson, who caught wolves with fish hooks; Samuel Askey, who slew ninety-eight wolves, and David Zimmerman, who drove the wolves out of Sugar Valley. There is plenty of glory, and an admiring posterity; there can be no prouder title than slayer of the last native wolf in Pennsylvania. Let us hail the names of Nelson, Dickinson, Razey and the rest as heroes of the chase!

III. THE LAST PACK.

A
S long ago as 1835 the packs of wolves in Central Pennsylvania showed signs of diminishing. In the Spring of that year the bodies of fifty wolves were found in a gully on Jack's Mountain, not far from Youngmanstown, after the snow had melted. The poor animals, weakened from lack of food, had huddled together for mutual protection, been engulfed in a snowbank, and perished. Hunting parties, trappers and poisoners wiped out a dozen packs in the Juniata, Seven Mountains, and Black Forest regions between 1835 and 1850. At the time of the first settlers packs of 500 were common; during the first half of the nineteenth century a pack containing fifty was considered a rarity. After 1850, a pack of twenty was considered unusual.* In the Divide Region of Clearfield County three packs, all of about twenty individuals lingered on until after 1880. In the Seven Mountains only one pack survived, the celebrated Black Avengers, as they were called by some, or the *Schwartzegeisht* by others. This pack always contained twenty black wolves and held its numbers until after 1880. It made its headquarters in Treaster Valley, Mifflin County, but ranged through the entire Seven Mountains country. There is no record that they ever did any great amount of damage to live

*Dr. W. J. McKnight, of Brookville, Pa., says: "In the middle of the last century large packs of wolves roamed a greater part of the state."

stock or game, although Dr. J. T. Rothrock says that
they were one of the causes for the scarcity of deer
in Treaster Valley. Very few of them were ever
captured by hunters or trappers. Dan Treaster, of
Treaster Valley, trapped a few each winter, but followed the old Indian policy of keeping the breeding
stock alive. Forest fires and lumbering, as well as
diminishment of food supply after the Seven Mountains became a noted hunters' rendezvous caused their
numbers to grow less. Clem Herlacher, who camped in Treaster Valley in 1892 and 1893, says that the
pack numbered about a dozen during those years. In
1898 the beds of thirteen wolves were discovered by
fishermen in Detwiler Hollow, in the Seven Mountains, evidently this same pack of "black boys." In
February, 1902, George Grenoble was followed by
three black wolves in a wood between Millheim and
Aaronsburg, in Penn's Valley. Wolves singly and in
pairs were tracked in the Seven Mountains during
the winters of 1903, 1904 and 1905. P. F. Conser,
a Millheim farmer, was working in one of his fields
with his son Harry, in March, 1908, when they saw a
black wolf trotting along in a southerly direction, evidently headed for the Seven Mountains. This gave
rise to the story that the wolves were returning to the
Seven Mountains. It is said that wolves barked in
Treaster Valley and High Valley during the Spring
of 1908. It is claimed that wolf tracks were noticed
in the Bare Meadows in the winter of 1909. But that
is the last heard of the Black Avengers. A pack of

JOHN VANATTA PHILLIPS, Chatham Run, Pa.
Mr. Phillips was a terror to the Wolves in Clinton County in the olden days

Centre County brown wolves was wiped out by Samuel Askey, of Snow Shoe, who killed ninety-eight between 1820 and 1845. A pack of brown wolves hung on in the Shade Mountain country, and ranged up to the White Deer Mountains until April, 1879.* Famished, they attacked some dogs belonging to a raft moored at the foot of Bald Eagle Mountain, near Muncy, but most of them were shot by raftsmen. That was the last heard of the pack, which was undoubtedly the last pack in that part of Pennsylvania. The three packs of brown wolves in Clearfield County were harassed by trappers, most of them being killed by Seth Iredell Nelson and his associates. By 1890 they were reduced to three or four scattering individuals. There was a big pack of grey wolves in McKean County during the first half of the nineteenth century. At times it numbered a hundred animals old and young. Settlements along the Allegheny divided it, and part ranged into Potter County. The bulk of the McKean County aggregation were slain or scattered by C. W. Dickinson, formerly of Norwich, but the remnant were killed after 1886 on Potato Creek and Kinzua Creek. The last of the Potter County band was killed by John Razey, of Sunderlinville, in 1890, who collected the bounty on its scalp. However, Mr. C. W. Dickinson claims, with good reason, in Chapter VIII, that this animal was Col. Parker's escaped coyote. The grey wolf which followed the last elk killed by Jim Jacobson at Roulette, Potter County, in No-

*Some authorities state that the date was 1869.

vember, 1875, was shot a few weeks later by Le Roy
Lyman, a wealthy farmer. There was a pack of grey
wolves in Blair and Cambria County, which ranged
into other more southerly counties, and another pack
of grey wolves in Somerset County, which inhabited
Laurel Ridge. These packs were being constantly re-
inforced by starving animals from West Virginia. The
almost total destruction by hunters of deer, wild turkeys, grouse and rabbits in the mountains of Southern
Pennsylvania, caused the breaking up of these wolfish
companies, perhaps forever.

IV. THREE KINDS OF WOLVES.

IT is certain that there were three kinds of wolves
in Pennsylvania, although they may have been
color phases of one species, *canis mexicanus
nubilis*. This might stand as a fact were it not that
there was a difference in localities inhabited by the
several varieties. While there may have been cases
where black wolves whelped grey or brown pups, and
inversely, yet the concensus of opinion of the old
hunters, and it is on their observations that this book
is written, is that the wolves of Pennsylvania bred re-
markably true to color. The largest variety, the grey
wolf, was found in Northern and in Southern Pennsylvania, or to be more exact in the counties of the
Northern and Southern tier. The brown wolf, small-
est in size, was the variety that formerly abounded in
the Blue Mountains, in the West Branch Valley, clear
to Clearfield County, and in the Western part of the
State. The grey and brown varieties were less wary
and were more quickly exterminated than the third
variety, which was midway in size between the two,
the black wolf, *or canis lycaon*. This animal strangely
enough inhabited the most limited ground for it was
seldom seen outside the confines of the Seven Mountains in Centre and Mifflin Counties. And in the
Seven Mountains the old hunters aver that there were
no wolves except black ones. The color of these
black wolves was subject to variation. Some were

jetty black, others a dusky black, or very dark brown, others jetty black or dusky black with somewhat lighter coloring on the under parts. Many of them had brown ears. That the black wolf was a separate variety is upheld by the fact that its general contour was different from the others. This will be seen exactly in chapter IV, by studying the descriptions and dimensions of the black wolves as differentiated from the other kinds. As far as intelligence went, the black wolf was far the superior of the others. It was susceptible of domestication, and would have made the ideal hunting dog of Pennsylvania.* Audubon in his "Quadrupeds of North America" says: "Once when we were traveling on foot not far from the southern boundary of Kentucky, we fell in with a Black Wolf, following a man with his rifle on his shoulder. On speaking with him about this animal he assured us that it was as tame and gentle as a dog, and that he had never met with a dog that could trail a deer better. We were so much struck with this account and the noble appearance of the wolf, that we offered him one hundred dollars for it, but the owner said he would not part with it for any price." What was the case in the West, was equally true in the Seven Mountains. One or two of the earliest hunters trained Black Wolves to act as

---

*Dr. W. J. McKnight in his "Pioneer Outline History of Northwestern Pennsylvania" states "the pioneer hunter would sometimes raise a wolf pup. This pup would be a dog in every sense of the word until about two years old, and then would be a wolf in all his acts."

SETH IREDELL NELSON, Round Island, Pa.
Born February 11, 1809; Died April 11, 1905
He killed a brown Wolf in Clearfield County in his 83rd year

hunting dogs and companions. These and wild black
wolves bred with dogs owned by pioneers, producing
a really worthy progeny. St. George Mivart has said
"hybrids between the dog and the wolf have proved to
be fertile, though for no long period." The writer re-
members that in his early boyhood about twenty years
ago he saw several of these wolf-dogs. They were intelligent and kindly, and highly prized by their owners,
farmers in some of the valleys adjacent to the Seven
Mountains. The craze for handsome sheep dogs or
collies which struck the valleys about this time resulted in ending the breeding of the wolfish dogs,
which to those not in sympathy with them, were tech-
nically mongrels, and they eventually disappeared.
There are probably few of them now in existence.
Their owners declared that they never showed the
slightest tendency to revert to a wild state. In September, 1898, the writer visited a farmer, who tilled
some back lots at the foot of the mountains on the
South side of Brush Valley. This old fellow, Abe
Royer by name, kept some turkeys, half wild, which
were the result of his tame turkey hens crossing with
wild gobblers which lived on the mountains back of
his cabin. He also kept several wolf-dogs. These
animals had orange and grey coloring not unlike collies, but had the shorter hair and longer legs of
wolves. There was no trace of black in their coloring, although their owner stated that their grand sire
had been a black wolf which coupled with a shepherd
bitch some eight years before when he was lumbering

in High Valley. He said that neither turkeys nor dogs had the least inclination to revert to the savage proclivities of their ancestors. If the grey wolves and the brown wolves had any of the admirable characteristics of their black relatives, the old hunters sayeth not. "Crafty and mean" is the general verdict expressed about the grey wolves, "nasty like little cur dogs," is the general run of remarks relative to the brown wolves. Doubtless these uncomplimentary characterizations are unjust to the animals, but they were certainly not up to the standard of the black wolves. If all are of one variety these attempts at specialization are hardly worth the time to read! At the same time it may show that color in animals has much to do with habitation, character and disposition. It may help to reveal the secret of why some men are blonde and others dark.

V. DESCRIPTION AND HABITS.

M R. C. W. DICKINSON, of Smethport, McKean
County, the greatest living Pennsylvania wolf
hunter, and a gentleman of intelligence and
education, makes the following comments anent our
native wolves:

"The peculiar traits of the wolf family are too
numerous to state in full here, but will give some of
the main points. The wolf is one of the most cunning and shrewd animals we know anything about.
They are the most difficult animal to catch in a trap
that we know anything about. If a wolf is caught
in a trap by bait and should happen to make
his escape, don't try to catch that wolf with
bait again, for life is too short to do it.
The only way to catch that wolf is to set traps in a
path where they travel occasionally. Don't use any
bait; if you do he will give that locality a wide berth.
If a wolf gets caught in a trap and happens to twist
his foot off, he must leave the pack or drove he belongs with. Whether they drive him away or whether
he leaves them because he can't stand the long jour-
neys they take is a question we can't answer. We
never saw an instance of a three footed wolf traveling with other wolves; he always goes alone; keeps
near the settlements. He may be in three or four
counties in three or four days and never kills but one
sheep at a time, and never goes back to that carcass

for a second meal. The man that sets traps by these carcasses fools away his time. Their chief food consists of deer meat, mutton, woodchucks, coons and rabbits; but they can be kept on any food that a dog will live on. They are quite bold in night-time but unmerciful cowards in daylight, that is, as far as the human family are concerned. They are not afraid of other wild animals. A lone wolf will kill any deer or drive away most any bear, and two wolves will put any bear to flight in a hurry. But they are awfully afraid of man in the day-time, but in nighttime will come within ten or twelve rods of a small campfire and howl for an hour or more. We never knew of them to attack a man or to show any signs of fight, not even around their dens where they had their young. Their mating season is from the 5th to the 15th of February, and they have their puppies from the 10th to 20th of April. The number of whelps at a litter is from five to twelve. I have caught a she-wolf with eleven breasts being nursed. The size of the whelps, which are born blind, and almost black in color, is about the same as common pups would be from a dog that would weigh from sixty to eighty pounds.* The time from mating to the time of birth is nine weeks, the same as our common dog. When the young wolves are two

---

*Mivart says: "The mammary glands are from six to ten in number, but the variation which is found in the Domestic Dog as regards this character may lead us to anticipate that it may not be a constant one in the wild species."

GARDEAU, PENNA.
Showing grave of Col. Noah Parker, an old-time Wolf Hunter
From a photograph by W. T. Clarke

or three weeks old, the two old ones do their heavy killing of sheep. The male wolf stays with the female from mating time until the young are grown and hunts for food as faithfully as the mother wolf. When the young are about ten weeks old the old ones take them from the den and begin to teach them to travel. After they leave the den they are a band of wanderers. They do not return to the den again that year. They are taught to wander and kill. By the time they are six months old they are great rangers and will travel as far in a night as the old ones care to go. During late September and October the woodchucks are denned up for winter, so the wolves will begin to slaughter sheep again, but at this season of the year the number of sheep killed is only about half compared with May and June. Their sheep killing is not confined to the two periods above mentioned, for they are liable to make a raid on sheep at any time. During the latter part of January the old wolves will take the young wolves to some locality from twenty to forty miles from the den. Here they will soon teach the young they have got to stay away from them. They must not follow after the old ones; if they do, they get roughly handled. As soon as the young are thoroughly convinced they have got to shift for themselves the old ones return to their den, and any wolf that dares to venture near that point has got to be able to whip that pair or he must hike for other quarters. A full grown Pennsylvania grey wolf is about as tall as a greyhound, and has a long nose,

quite slim; he has large tusks, a fine set of teeth, a
mouth split well back; he has a treacherous rolling
eye, very keen; he is heavily built through the butt
of jaws; ears about four inches long, inclined to be
thick and stand up on his head like a fox's ears. He
is quite deep through the chest and well cut up in the
flanks. He is thin through the chest, body and hams.
The shape of his body after being skinned is similar
to the body of a fox, only very much larger. His hair
or fur is long but not coarse. It gives him a shaggy
appearance. His tail is long and shaggy. A full
grown wolf of this species will weigh from 60 to 80
pounds. There have been some larger ones caught in
this section weighing as high as ninety pounds. I saw
a western timber wolf in the Zoo at Buffalo, N. Y., in
March, 1914, and it seemed to me slightly bigger than
the grey wolf of Northern Pennsylvania. But it
may have been better fed. Their main hold on
a sheep or deer (except a buck deer with antlers)
is the throat, which they will hang to, giving the
animal a few violent shakes which will make their
necks creak until the animal stops struggling, then
he will let go. If he is a cripple he will pro-
ceed to take a meal, but if he belongs to a den
where there are young whelps he will look for a
chance to kill another sheep, and if he can't see any
more to kill he will take a meal and hike and won't
return to any of the dead sheep again or visit this
section again that season, unless he can come in on
the opposite side of that field, then it is fresh mutton

for him. He will not visit any of the old carcasses. The wolf is very strong, quick and active. If a lone wolf gets up to a buck deer with antlers the wolf will juke and dodge around the buck until he gets a snap or two at that buck's gambrel joints. At a single snap he will have one leg of that buck useless and a snap or two at the other gambrel joint, and that buck's hind legs are useless. He will stand on his gambrels instead of his hind feet. Now he is an easy prey for that wolf. Just one throat hold and that buck is a dead deer. The only good trait of the wolf is the old male will not leave the mother wolf to take care of her young; he is always with her, death being the only thing to separate them. Still many men think the wolf ought to have been protected by law. Not any of that for me, but I think that the bounty laws are superfluous and a waste of the State's money." These grey wolves were probably the type which Mr. S. N. Rhoads called *canis Mexicanus nubilis*. In size they were the largest of the Pennsylvania wolves. In Williams' Civil and Natural History of Vermont, published in 1797, the weight of a Vermont wolf is given as 92 pounds. A large specimen of the European wolf mentioned in the same work is given as 69 pounds 8 ounces. Harlan, in his Pennsylvania Natural History, evidently refers to the brown wolf when he says: "The wolf in Pennsylvania is reddish brown color, the hair being tipped with black, but especially so over the fore shoulders and sides." Bartram in his natural history notes says: "The wolves of Pennsylvania are a yellowish brown color." This is the variety which is called in Trego's "Geography of Pennsylvania" *lupus occidentalis*. A better name would be *canis occidentalis*. Audubon gives the measurements of a black wolf as follows: Length of head and body 3 feet 2 inches, tail vertebra, 11 inches; tail vertebra, including fur, 1 foot 1 inch; length of ear, 3 inches. C. W. Dickinson gives the length of the ear of a Pennsylvania wolf as 4 inches; "tail very long." These animals being noted for their long trailing tails were called by the old settlers "the long-tailed hunters." Others among the old-timers called them the "Mountain Nightingales." A black wolf caught in Penn's Valley, in Centre County, Pa., about 1857, measured, whole length, 4 feet 4 inches; tail, 1 foot; length of ear, 2 inches. The ears of this wolf were very narrow, the nose was more pointed and the tail not quite so long as the grey wolves from the Northern part of the State. The black wolf is known scientifically as *canis lycaon*. The measurements of a brown wolf taken in Sugar Valley before the Civil War is given as, length from point of nose to root of tail, 2 feet 11 inches; tail, 1 foot one inch. The measurements of a Western grey wolf are given as, nose to origin of tail, 4 feet 3¾ inches; length of trunk of tail, 1 foot 1 inch; ear 3¾ inches. These are singularly like the measurements of the grey wolves noted by C. W. Dickinson in Northern Pennsylvania. While it may be possible that the three varieties of wolves found in Penn-

JACOB P. HAMERSLEY, Renovo, Pa.
Slayer of the last Wolf in Clinton County

sylvania were all variations of the one species they
exhibit a marked difference. The grey wolf of the
Northern Counties was the biggest and strongest variety, his prevailing color was dark grey, his head and
jaws large, his ears long and pointed. The brown
wolf of the Eastern and Central part of the State was
about the size of the animal which Audubon called
the "Red Texas wolf," or most likely the size of a
male coyote. It varied in color from a yellowish to a
reddish brown. It had smaller and squarer ears than
the grey wolf of the North. The black wolf, which
seldom if ever was found outside of the Seven Mountains was slightly larger than the brown wolf, more
rangy in build, with long but narrower ears, and a
tremendous length of nose. It varied in color from
a sooty grey, or hyena color, to a jet, shiny black. Its
tail was often so devoid of hair, especially in Summer, as to resemble a black curved stick. It was the
swiftest runner of all the three varieties. It was very
moderate in its diet and seldom attacked sheepfolds.
It would have been an ideal animal for coursing with
dogs. Audubon gives the height of a western grey
wolf as two feet five inches. C. W. Dickinson
says the Pennsylvania grey wolf was the height
of a greyhound. A Pennsylvania black wolf was
said to be "about the height of a half-breed
shepherd dog." A Pennsylvania brown wolf "resembled in height and general appearance a small-
sized foxhound." From these meagre pen-pictures
perhaps those interested in the wolves of the Key-

stone State can evolve a series of portraits. It is a shame on our naturalists that none of these wolves were secured for our various museums or Zoological Gardens. Regarding the barking of Pennsylvania wolves Dr. McKnight, who often heard them, says: "For the benefit of those who have never heard a wolf's musical soiree, I will state here that one wolf leads off in a long tenor and the whole pack joins in the chorus."

VI. FORMER PREVALENCE.

O NE of the first enactments made by William Penn
during his second visit to Pennsylvania in 1699
was to have a bounty placed upon the scalps of
wolves.* The great Quaker interested himself in the
matter reluctantly as he was a great believer in the
conservation of fur-bearing animals.† But a couple of
cold winters had set the wolves to howling about the
very outskirts of Philadelphia, and something had to
be done to quiet the public clamor. Calves, pigs and
sheep, taken in some instances by two-footed thieves
no doubt were charged against the wolves, so they
had to suffer. Hundreds of wolves were slain to col-
lect the bounty. At first the numbers did not
seem to decrease, and a cry was made to double
the bounty. This was done in some localities through
private liberality. At the time of Penn's death in
1718, wolves were practically exterminated east of
Lancaster. Of course they were plentiful still in the
Blue Mountains and in the Lehigh and Pocono regions until a century later. But by the date of Penn's

---

*At a Court held at Chester, Oct. 2, 1695, it was stated
that "there are several wolves heads to pay for," showing
that there was a bounty on wolves' heads as early as 1695.
In 1705 wolves had so increased in numbers about Philadelphia that an Act was passed in that year for the killing of wolves (Col. Rec. Vol. II., pp. 212, 231). The amount
paid was 10 shillings for a dog wolf, 15 shillings for a
she-wolf.

†See Clarkson's "Memoirs of William Penn." Vol. II.

demise they were known no more in the fertile farm-
ing regions in what is now Montgomery, Chester,
Lancaster and York Counties. At the time of the
French and Indian war, when the chain of forts along
the Blue Mountains were attacked in 1755, wolves
were present in large companies. While there is no
record or tradition extant of their having molested
human beings, they proved a source of complaint as
considerable as the redmen. Wolves and panthers,
as well as the Indians, pillaged the farms at the base
of the Blue Mountains, carrying off much stock.
Twenty years later they were still numerous along the
Blue Mountains, and women whose husbands had
gone to the front in the Revolutionary war complain-
ed that there was no one to guard stock and children
from packs of hungry wolves. One woman, Mrs.
Barbara Schwartz, wife of a Revolutionary soldier,
shot three wolves which had attacked her watch dog,
the shooting occurring in her front yard near the
present town of Schubert. After the war the returned soldiers formed hunting parties so that by the
close of the eighteenth century these savage animals
were seen no more east of the Blue Mountains.*
Until the middle of the nineteenth century they were
prevalent in Franklin, Adams, Cumberland, Perry,
Schuylkill, Luzerne and adjoining counties to the
North. In 1845 or thereabouts they are described as

---

*According to H. Hollister's "Lackawanna Valley"
they were alarmingly prevalent in the Lackawanna County
in 1798.

CLEMENT F. HERLACHER, Loganton, Pa.
Who hunted Wolves in Clearfield County in the early '80s
From a photograph by Eliza Huntley
Taken on the famous Hunter's return from the Wolf country

being very numerous in the Wyoming and Tom-
hicken Valleys. They were still found by the hundreds in the Seven Mountains, and to the South
of them, and in Potter, McKean and Clearfield Counties. They were exterminated in the
West Branch Valley, except as stragglers, about
this time. The celebrated Black Wolf, which reg-
ularly followed the packet boats on the West
Branch Canal, from Williamsport to Lock Haven
at night, was killed during the great flood of
1847 by Mike Curts, where the old woolen mill now
stands in Antes Gap.* "Black Headed Bill" Williams, old-timer and veteran Bucktail, of Pine
Station, Clinton County, says that the last time
he heard a wolf call on the Round Top back of his
home was in the Fall of 1863, when he was home
from the army on a furlough. Wolves from Sugar
Valley often appeared on the Round Top, which rises
directly South of Mr. Williams' home, long after they
had ceased to breed in its rocky caverns. Wolves in
Clearfield County were plentiful on Mosquito Creek,
in 1880, according to Leonard Johnson, formerly a
well-known lumberman. They kept up such a howling at night, and such a scampering around the horse
stables in a camp where he was employed, that the
horses would hardly be fit for work the next day, so
terrified were the poor equines. Wolves were

---

*Mrs. Lanks, who as a small girl saw the wolf and
alarmed the neighborhood, said it was black with wide
brown bars. She has been called the "Little Red Riding
Hood of the West Branch."

numerous on Potato Creek in McKean County up to about that same year. The old packs, such as had marooned Dan Treaster in his barn in Treaster Valley, Mifflin County, up to about 1850, were about run out in the Seven Mountains by 1880. As individuals wolves could not thrive. They relied on company for the success of their hunting operations, and they apparently lacked the courage to forage alone. In Penn's time packs of five hundred wolves had been noticed. Peter Pentz, who died in 1812, was once followed by a pack of two hundred, which was con sidered an unusually large number at that time.

VII. THE BIGGEST WOLF.

FROM "Old" Nicholas, a respectable Indian well known along the Coudersport Pike comes the story of the killing of the biggest Pennsylvania wolf. As may be supposed, it was a grey wolf. The slayer was none other than the famous half-breed hunter, Jim Jacobson, who brought to earth the last elk in Pennsylvania, and some say the last twelve elks slain in the Commonwealth. But the most remarkable part of the narrative is that this intrepid hunter was but ten years of age at the time of this matchless exploit! The biggest wolf was killed by the "littlest" hunter. Jim Jacobson, or to be more exact, Samuel Jimmerson Jacobson, was born at New Bergen, now Carter Camp, in Potter County, in 1848. The parental shack stood, it is said, on the site of Charles Schreibner's barn. His father, Jacob Jacobson, was a native of Sweden Hill, not far from Coudersport, while his mother was Mary Jimmerson, daughter of King Jimmerson, a Seneca chieftain, who was said to be a son of Mary Jemison, the justly celebrated "White Woman of the Genessee." Jacob Jacobson was of Swedish extraction and died in 1852. It was during the month of April, 1858, that the now historic "Spring Blizzard," a snow storm of unprecedented severity, occurred.* Wild beasts of all kinds were

---

*According to the Clinton County Times this blizzard occurred in the latter part of April, 1854.

driven from the forests, frantic with hunger. It appeared that the boy's mother had gone to Oleona to spend the day, leaving the future nimrod in charge of the shanty. The ground was covered with snow, and it was bitterly cold. The lad, who was looking out of the window, noticed a large animal walking about at the edge of the brook. Boldly he came out of the house, as he thought that the creature, to judge from its color, was some one's stray calf. When he got within twenty feet of it he saw, to his dismay, that it was a gigantic grey wolf. He did not falter; turning on his heel, he fled up the slippery bank, and into the house, never once looking back. As he turned to slam the heavy plank door he saw that the brute had been at his heels. He had never heard of such conduct on the part of a wild beast and determined to be avenged. Slamming and bolting the door, he took down his late father's firearm which hung over a small daguerrotype of that worthy gentleman. It was always kept loaded for just such an emergency, and now it had come. Softly opening the window he took aim at the wolf, which stood sniffing at the door-sill. There was a loud report, and the savage beast turned a back somersault into the yard—dead. The tiny boy had shot it through the jugular vein. Tieing it up by its hind feet to the clothes-line, he left it until his mother's return. Accompanied by several redskins, among them Old Nicholas, Tall Chief and Johnny Shongo, she reached the shanty about nightfall. Imagine her horror to see the hideous carcass

ARMS OF SAMUEL MICHAEL QUINN
Famous Pennsylvania Wolf Hunter

Description—A hand couped at the wrist, grasping a sword, two serpents erect and inspecting each other, two crescents. Crest—a wolf's head erased.

hanging just inside the crude gate. Jimmy was watching for her, and ran forward, rifle in hand. The Indians were delighted to see that the half-breed boy possessed such courage, and danced and sang with glee. Then the carcass was measured. It was just one inch over six feet from tip to tip, and its estimated weight was 100 pounds. The tail, measured separately, was exactly two feet. The famous "Beaver Dam Wolf" killed in Blair County, in 1907, according to enthusiastic chroniclers, measured less than six feet, and weighed eighty-four pounds. The hide was stretched and cured according to the formulas of the redmen and sent as a relic to Ole Bull, who during his residence near New Bergen had befriended the Indian widow and her Norse-blooded son. Unfortunately the great violinist was on a tour when the skin reached New York, and it became lost before he returned to claim it. It is said that he wrote a note of thanks to the lad, which the celebrated hunter preserved to his dying day. This early triumph decided the career of Jim Jacobson. He became a hunter, devoting practically his entire time to the pursuit of big game. Though jealous of his reputation as a nimrod, he was modest and unobtrusive, and others claimed titles and honors that were justly his. But his record as the slayer of the last elk and biggest wolf in Pennsylvania are firmly established.

VIII.   A WHITE WOLF IN SUGAR VALLEY.

'SQUIRE GEORGE WAGNER, who died at his comfortable mountain-top home in Rosecrans, Clinton County, a few months ago in his 74th year, used to relate an interesting story of a large white wolf which plagued the early inhabitants of Sugar Valley. This animal, because of its unusual color, was shunned by the rest of the pack, being compelled to lead a solitary existence. Its isolated life made it misanthropic and added to its cruelty, for it was the terror of the stockmen for several years. Hunting parties were organized, traps and snares of all kinds were set out, but it escaped them, creating havoc among sheep and calves. Of course the amount of damage done by it was greatly exaggerated by the old-timers, but that is neither here nor there. One night Michael Schreckengast, an old farmer living near Tylersville heard a commotion in his barn, and hurrying out reached the door just in time to meet the white wolf emerging, his jaws covered with blood. The aged German slammed the door on the brute, catching it by the tail. He threw a plough-share against the door and ran to the house for his rifle. By the time he got back the wolf had gone, leaving his bushy tail wedged in the door. Old Schreckengast used the tail for many years as a plume on the cock-horse of his spike team. After all methods had failed to rid the valley of the white

wolf Jacob Reeser, an old settler, suggested calling
the aid of George Wilson, a veteran of the War of
1812, who lived across the Northern Mountains at
McElhattan. Wilson, who survived to the age of
106 years, had shot several "spook wolves" with silver bullets. On his way to Lock Haven one day
Reeser had the good fortune to meet Granny McGill,
a reputed witch. This grand old lady of eighty-six
years, suggested that before calling in Wilson a home
remedy be tried. It consisted in securing a black
lamb, born in the Fall of the year, in the dark of the
moon, and tying it near a spring trap. After much
difficulty such a lamb was found in Isaac Cooper's
flock, and tied by the trap, at the summit of Mount
Lookout, near Loganton, where the wolf's den was
located. The plan worked like a charm the very first
time. After devouring the defenseless lamb the
white wolf began smelling at the trap, perhaps in
search of more good things. It sprang, catching him
by the nose. In the morning he was found by the
hunters and beaten to death with clubs. Nehemiah
Basom got the pelt, which served as a hearth rug in
his home near Carroll for a long time. Few strangers
would believe that it was a wolf's hide. The long
white hair and bob tail made it resemble the pelt of
an Angora goat. Unfortunately the head was not
mounted with the skin, but was set up on a pole
above old Mr. Reeser's sheep-fold, like a murderer
on London Bridge. It remained there until a heavy
wind blew it down, and it was eaten by hogs. Chil-

dren were afraid to pass the sheep-pen after dark
while the wolf's head was on the pole. Truthful
youngsters declared that it snapped its jaws and that
its eyes flashed green light on particularly rough
nights. No wolves came near the pen while the head
was in evidence. A week later a pack pillaged the
pen to the tune of ten early lambs. Another report
has it that they were stolen by trout fishermen and
roasted at an orgy held in the Gotschall Hollow. A
female sheep dog owned by a farmer in the East end
of the Valley, during the hey-day of the white wolf
gave birth to a litter of tailless white pups. These
were immediately put to death, as it was feared they
would bring bad luck. A preacher met the white wolf
in the graveyard at Brungard's Church, and the animal ran out of the gate yelping piteously. It acted,
the preacher said, like a yellow cur that had had
boiling water poured on it, or as one old free-thinker*
put it, "it feared the sky-pilot like the devil would
holy water." After it was skinned, its flesh was
found to be full of scars, the result of conflicts with
brown and black wolves, which hated it as much as did
the human residents of the region.

*Dennis Haley, of Robbins' Hollow.

GEORGE SCOTT SMITH, of Elk County, Pa.
Slayer of 500 Wolves in the Pennsylvania forests
Photo loaned by Dr. W. J. McKnight, Brookville, Pa.

IX. DISAPPEARANCE.

I T may be of some satisfaction to the admirers of
the wolfish race in Pennsylvania to know
that their disappearance was not due to the
hunters. Comparatively few were trapped or
shot, as the bounty records will show.* Man,
however, was indirectly responsible for their passing out of sight. By destroying their food
supply they were compelled to die of starvation
or strike for a new country. The prevalence
of wolves in McKean County in the late seventies was due to their desire to pass through there
to New York State. The open country North of
Alleghany and Cattaraugus Counties, in New York,
made it impossible for them to reach the Adirondack
wilderness, and they congregated in the vast forests
of original timber in Potato Creek, where they
starved to death and were slaughtered or poisoned.
The black wolves of the Seven Mountains made a
similar effort to reach the North Woods. David
Frantz, a celebrated wolf hunter, who lived near
Coburn, Centre County, said that in 1898 and 1899
wolf tracks were observed across Penn's Valley,
passing in a northerly direction. Wolves were seen

---

*Rev. Joseph Doddridge, in his "Notes," ascribes the
rapid dimunition of wolves in Pennsylvania to hydropho-
bia. He relates several instances where settlers who were
bitten by wolves perished miserably from that terrible
disease.

43

and tracked in Brush Valley, Sugar Valley and along the Coudersport Pike in the winters of those years. One or two hung about Henry Campbell's saw mill, near Haneyville, in the early part of 1898. Wolves were seen in Penn's Valley in 1900, 1901 and 1902. In 1908 a black wolf was observed traveling South towards the Seven Mountains. How far North these wolves traveled can only be conjectured. Doubtless some of them get as far as the Northern border of the Black Forest, there turning back at the vast stretch of arable land ahead of them. Their instinct told them to go North; for some reason they did not travel South. All the native wolves of Southern Pennsylvania were grey, and between these and the black variety existed a marked antipathy. Perhaps they dreaded going South, and encountering their old-time foes. In the North there were no native wolves after 1890, and in that respect the way was clear. In the Southern counties a few native wolves hung on after 1890, but they were constantly re-inforced by wanderers from West Virginia and Maryland. Be it as it may, the two or three black wolves which remained were back in the Seven Mountains in 1908, and doubtless died of starvation during the following year. They were probably the same as left that region ten years before, and were therefore very aged specimens at the time of their return. Dr. C. Hart Merriam in his remarkable treatise on the mammals of the Adirondack region, in speaking of the disappearance of wolves in the North Woods says: "In

BILL LONG, 1794—1880
The King of Pennsylvania Hunters; Slayer of 2000 Pennsylvania Wolves
Born in Berks County, Died in Clearfield County

Photo loaned by Dr. W. J. McKnight, Brookville, Pa.

the year 1871 New York State put a bounty on their
scalps, and it is a most singular coincidence that a
great and sudden decrease in their numbers took
place at about that time. What became of them is a
g.cat and, to me, inexplicable mystery, for it is known
that but few were slain. There is but one direction
in which they could have escaped, and that is through
Clinton County into lower Canada. In so doing they
would have been obliged to pass around the North
end of Lake Champlain and cross the River Riche-
lieu and before reaching the extensive forests would
have had to travel long distances through tolerably
well- settled portions of country. And there is no
evidence that they made any such journey." Doubtless more Adirondack wolves were killed than were
born, and like the wild pigeons which were similarly
affected, they had to come to an end. In other words
the old ones all died out about the same year. In
Pennsylvania it was rather a case of starvation than
destruction as the result of relentless hunting. In
the Adirondacks deer were plentiful at the time the
wolves disappeared. In Pennsylvania when the black
wolves made their ineffectual break for the North
wild life was at its lowest ebb in the Seven Mountains. The bulk of the original pine and hemlock
was gone, disastrous forest fires were annually lay-
ing waste vast areas, hunters and trappers were
everywhere. The active measures of the Forestry
Department, which checked wasteful fires, and the
wise foresight of the Game Commission which en-

forced game laws on the small lot of wild life which
remained, came too late for the wolves. When the
remnant returned, they were very old, and may all
possibly have been of the same sex. Mr. C. W. Dickinson says that wolves being cannibals may have had
much to do with their decrease. Whatever the
cause, they succumbed, and the race ceased to exist.
Although the writer has not been in the Seven Mountains as frequently in the past few years as formerly,
and would gladly stand corrected, he has been un-
able to find the slightest evidence of wolves in the
Seven Mountains since 1909. These were the last
native wolves in Pennsylvania. They made a gal-
lant stand, but the destruction of their food supply
and forest fires sent them into oblivion. Dan
Treaster, one of the noblest of wolf hunters, when
asked why he did not enlist outside aid to rid Treaster
Valley of wolves stated: "Destroy their food supply
and they will go soon enough." There was ample
verification of his prophesy.

CHARLES IVES and THEODORE PIERCE
Slayers of the Last Native Grey Wolf in Northern Pennsylvania, 1888
(*From a tintype taken shortly before the time of their great exploit*)

X. WOLF HUNTING IN PENNSYLVANIA.

By C. W. Dickinson, Smethport, McKean County, the Greatest Living Wolf Hunter.

A S to the killing of the last grey wolf in Pennsylvania, I can only state that I believe the last grey, or timber wolf as they are called in many sections, was killed in McKean County in the latter part of September or fore part of October in 1886.* Two boys from Bradford came up to Mt. Jewett, a small town along the N. Y. & Erie R. R., about three miles South of the famous Kinzua Viaduct. The boys got off the train at Mt. Jewett, went to the Nelson Hotel, which was kept by a man by the name of W. Wallace Brewer, who by the way was an old hunter and trapper here. The boys stated they were going down to the old Beaver Meadows to spend a week in search of big game, and they each wanted to get a pint of whiskey. Mr. Brewer informed them they were too young to get any liquor, and advised them to go back to Bradford, as big game was scarce in that locality and said he thought they stood as much of a chance to find a gold mine as they did to kill anything larger than a porcupine. The boys were not in a mood to be discouraged; they shouldered their knapsacks and guns and started for the old Beaver Meadows, which are about a mile and a half from Mt. Jewett, on the Kinzua Creek. When they

---

*Charles Ives, one of the party, gives the date as 1888.

were about half way to the Meadows they heard a
rifle shot up the valley about a mile away. The boys
took off their packs to rest a few minutes, and one of
them remarked, "Let's keep watch for a few minutes
in the direction of the rifle shot, as we may see something coming this way." Just then one said: "What
is that coming?" The animal came within about eight
rods, jumped on an old log and stopped and looked
back toward the point where the rifle report was
heard. One of the lads raised his rifle and fired and
the game disappeared. The boys went out to see
what had become of the animal they had shot at.
When they got to the place, there lay some kind of
animal, but what it was they did not know, so they
shouldered their knapsacks and returned to the hotel,
dragging the animal, as they wanted to find out what
it was. On reaching the hotel one of the boys called
on Mr. Brewer to come out and tell them what kind
of an animal they had killed. As soon as Mr. Brewer
saw the animal he exclaimed: "Well, well, boys, you
have got a prize. You have got a genuine wolf, only
he has got but three feet. The left hind foot was miss-
ing. But that wolf has got more dead sheep to his
credit than any wolf ever had before." Mr. Brewer
told the boys what to do to get the bounty on the
wolf, which at that time was $25.00. Now, I am sure
this was the last grey or timber wolf caught or killed
anywhere in this section of Pennsylvania, for all the
Potter County or Blair County wolf stories, which I
will explain later on. There is a section of this State

which used to be known as the wildcat district, which
included Potter County, Cameron County, Clearfield
County, Jefferson County, Elk County, Forest County
and McKean County, which was the last home and
breeding places of the grey wolf. Now, we say grey
wolf because this was the only species of wolf we had
in that section for the last 100 years, except a few
coyotes that were brought into McKean from the
Western plains. We never had any black or brown
wolves in this locality, not for the last 100 years. It
is true there was a little difference in the color of
some of them; some would be a shade lighter or a
shade darker than others, but this variation in color
was very small when compared with the medium
color. As the lumber trade was carried on more ex-
tensively in all of the above named Counties except
McKean, in which the trade was carried on only
in a small way along the Allegheny River and Potato
Creek, it left the Southern part of this County, the
Northern part of Cameron County and the Northern
part of Elk County a virgin forest, only traversed by
hunters and trappers. In this section the wolves had
their last pow-wow. From 1850 until the last one
was killed the number of sheep killed by wolves
will never be known, but the toll was heavy.
To give the reader something of an idea of
these losses, will state some of my near neighbors' losses. A man who lived within a half mile of
my father, wishing to make some of his relatives in
the middle Western States a visit, rented his farm and

stock to a man by the name of C. P. Rice, the stock
being ten or twelve head of cattle and about forty
sheep, giving Rice possession April 1, 1868. About
the 20th of May two wolves came in and killed fourteen sheep for Mr. Rice in one night, and fifteen days
later they came back and killed fourteen more, making a loss of twenty-eight sheep. Besides this loss,
Mr. Rice lost about one dozen of the orphan lambs,
making his total loss about forty sheep and lambs. In
1869, about the 10th of May, wolves came in and
killed eleven sheep for C. A. Burdick in a single
night. Mr. Burdick's farm adjoined my father's
farm on the West side. Five days later the wolves
came back and killed the two that they did not get
the first night. Mr. Burdick had thirteen ewes and
none of them had dropped their lambs yet, so the only
way to estimate his loss would be to say he lost all he
had. Every farmer that kept sheep had to contribute
to "Mr. Wolf." Wolves were very cunning when
they killed a farmer's sheep. They would not return
to get another meal of the dead sheep, but would
make a raid on the live ones. It seemed to be their
delight to kill as long as they could find anything to
kill. And it looks as if they were afraid to return to
the dead animal for fear of getting their toes pinched.
This cunning trait of theirs made it extremely difficult to trap them. Nevertheless, from 1865 until the
last one was killed we waged a relentless war on
them. The winter of 1874-75 was a hummer. The
snow was very deep and the mercury went from 30

CHIEFTAIN

Famous Irish Wolfhound, owned by General Roger D. Williams, Lexington, Ky.

Photo published by courtesy of owner

to 38 degrees below zero many times. Two brothers, Mike and Dick Griffin, lived in the Southern part of Keating Township. They lost a yearling steer. They drew the steer out into the woods and skinned it. One of the men went past the carcass of the steer one day and noticed that a pack of wolves were making nightly visits to the carcass for their meals, as he noticed a well traveled path where they came down from the mountains for their nightly meal, and take the same path to the mountains. The men purchased a bottle of strychnine and poisoned the carcass. The wolves returned that night and ate their last meal. They went back into the mountains. The men followed the trail some distance and got discouraged as the snow was very deep. They gave up. They thought the poison no good because it did not kill almost instantly. They found after a while that the poison would kill their neighbor's dogs and even kill crows that fed on that carcass. There is not a doubt in my mind but what that was the last meal any of that bunch ever ate. ·In June, 1877, the writer found where wolves had killed a deer. It being in a locality where young cattle were liable to feed, making it dangerous to set traps, we decided to use poison. None of the brutes came back after eating one meal of the poisoned meat. In December, 1878, wolves killed six sheep for a neighbor. We tied one of the dead sheep on a hand-sled, drew it back into the woods about one mile, following the trail where the wolves had come in. We poisoned this carcass to kill. In about two weeks we had a severe thaw; the snow all went off; the ground was as bare as summer time for about two weeks. During this time the wolves came and cleaned up the carcass of that sheep. This was in January, 1879, and since that time the writer has not seen or heard of a wolf track being seen in snow in this part of Pennsylvania, except the two cripples which were both killed in this County later on. In the seventies the writer got the left hind foot of a wolf in a steel trap. The wolf had got the body of the trap over a knot on an old log. As the trap could not turn around the swivel in the chain it was useless and he twisted his foot off at the ankle joint and got away. Now, this was the same wolf the two boys killed on the Kinzua Creek in 1886. A man by the name of Albert Goodwin took a fore foot off of a wolf in a bear trap in the fall of 1877. This wolf was caught by Zack Carl in 1881 or 1882, and the only track seen of a grey wolf in this part of the State by any hunter or trapper after Carl caught the one he got, was the tracks of the wolf with a hind foot off. And after the boys killed that one on the Kinzua, there has not a single track or sign of a grey wolf been seen in Northwestern Pennsylvania by any hunter or trapper. Now, at the date of the killing of the wolf in 1886, the large piece of forest in this locality, starting at Gardeau, in the W. N. Y. & P. R. R., traveling a little South of West to Johnsonburg, was about forty miles; starting at Clermont, in this county, and go in a Southerly direction through this same forest to St. Mary's, in Elk County, the distance is about twenty-five miles. At the time of the above dates there were probably two dozen hunters' cabins located at various points in this forest, and they were usually occupied from the latter part of October until December 31st, and none of them ever reported seeing a wolf track after the Fall and fore part of Winter of 1885, and for four or five years prior to 1885 they saw no wolf signs, only of one or the other of these wolves which had a foot off. Now, the writer is certain there was not a single wolf raised in this section in the last thirty-four or thirty-five years. If a pair of wolves had raised a litter of whelps anywhere in this section the damage to the owners of sheep for a radius of thirty miles would have created excitement enough so it would be known for a hundred miles around that neighborhood. As to the Potter County wolf story, we would like to state some facts in regard to this statement. While we remember very well of reading the account of this at the time it happened, we wish to state a few facts in regard to this subject. Col. Noah Parker, an old hunter, who lived at Gardeau in the Southeastern part of Norwich Township close to the Potter County line, went to Colorado in 1884 for the express purpose of killing an elk, and when he returned from Colorado he brought home a female coyote. He made a dog house for it and chained it up, as he dared not allow it to run loose. Later on he bred this coyote to a dog he kept and the coyote raised a litter of pups, but they proved to be a lot of thieves. They would kill sheep or poultry and steal all the meat around the premises unless it was under a lock and key, and in due time they were all killed off for being common thieves. About two months before Mr. Razey caught his wolf, Col. Parker's coyote broke her collar and made her escape. She was seen a number of times before Mr. Razey caught the Potter County "wolf," but never seen after. The wolf that Mr. Razey caught was a female, and as Mr. Razey said it was a small sized wolf he caught, we will bet a bushel of bull frogs to a pint of cider that the wolf Mr. Razey caught was Col. Parker's escaped coyote. The writer was well acquainted with Mr. Parker and had a number of talks with him about this matter, and Mr. Parker told me that he had talked with Razey about the wolf he caught and he (Parker) was dead sure that Razey's wolf was his escaped coyote, and as Mr. Parker expressed himself, he said: "I am damned glad that Razey caught that coyote, for I was afraid I would have a bill of damages to pay for her depredations." We both thought that Potter County was better able to pay Mr. Razey the $25 bounty than to have some poor farmer lose twice that amount in sheep. Now, with due respect to Mr. Razey, we must say that we believe that he was honest in his opinion that he had caught a wolf, for the following reason: Take a small size grey wolf and a large coyote and we don't believe that Potter County has got a man today that could tell which one

VZANYI

Pennsylvania-bred, Russian Wolfhound, owned by J. Bailey Wilson, Lansdowne, Pa.

was wolf or coyote. There are only two points to judge from, the coyote is not as strong or heavy through the butt of the jaws, and his tail is two inches or more shorter than the tail of a grey wolf of the same size. During the latter part of the 'nineties, a man living in the City of Bradford, Pa., had a cage of young coyotes sent him by a friend in one of the Western States. He fixed a pen in his yard, put the five coyotes in it, and after a couple of years these coyotes broke jail one night and all made their escape. One of them was killed the next morning in a neighbor's hen house, where he had killed half the poultry in the house. The next they were seen was near Rixford and Duke Center, where two of them were shot while they were killing sheep. The next place the two remaining ones were seen was on the farm of L. J. Gallup, in Liberty Township (which adjoins Potter County). They came into Mr. Gallup's sheep pasture in mid-day and killed a sheep. Mr. Gallup saw them kill the sheep. He took his rifle out and shot one of them; the other one made his escape, and the only thing we have ever heard (until recently) of the lone coyote was an item we saw about seven years ago in the WilliamsportGrit which stated that a wolf had been killed in Blair County, where there had not been a wolf seen for forty years. At the time we read about this Blair County wolf we were of the opinion that if anything like a wolf had been killed in that locality it was the last one of the five coyotes that made their escape in Bradford. We saw an item clipped from the Altoona Tribune of January 21, 1914, giving an account of the killing of the Beaver Dam wolf, and as the writer of that article gave such a glowing account of the event, we can't see why he should have been so shy about his being known. Now, we challenge Mr. County Contributor, Hollidaysburg, to produce any authority to show where a den of young grey wolves were raised in the State of Pennsylvania, outside of McKean County, within the last forty-five years. Next, we challenge you to show us a single citizen of Blair County who ever saw a wolf outside of a cage in Blair County. Dare you come out and state when or about what time the last bounty was paid on a wolf in your County. Dare you state that you ever saw a grey wolf outside of a cage or zoo or park in Pennsylvania or anywhere else. Now, Mr. County Contributor, we know that there has not been a single den of young wolves raised within this State in the last thirty-six years. Had that Beaver Dam coyote been a grey wolf, he could not have been less than 29 years old! At that age would he have had as nice teeth as you saw? Now, Mr. Contributor, will you tell us what is the natural age of a wolf. In your description of the Beaver Dam animal, you could not give any better description of a coyote if you had one to look at. That short bushy tail you speak of is about the only sure mark that you can rely on to tell a large coyote from a small grey wolf. The old-time hunters in this locality used to call our wolves the "long tailed hunt-

ers." Then, again, you say the people thought this
animal was a big grey fox. Just think of that; one
of our Pennsylvania wolves is eight or ten times
heavier than a fox. You sav a large dog was badly
chewed up by this animal. Now, Mr. Contributor,
we will wager $100 that there is not a dog in Blair
County that could catch a big Pennsylvania grey wolf
in an all night chase. And we will wager $100 more
that you haven't got any two dogs in the County
that can whip one of them. We will put up another
$100 that you have not got a dog in your County that
can catch a coyote, and we don't believe you have a
dog that can whip a coyote. You say young Mr.
Moore saw this animal jumping and snapping at the
throats of his father's sheep. Now, Mr. Contributor,
if one of our Pennsylvania wolves had made a single
snap at a sheep's throat, that sheep would have been
a dead one before Mr. Moore could get his revolver
out of his pocket, to say nothing about shooting, for
one of our wolves would kill a sheep as quickly as a
cat could kill a rat. We have seen this trick done and
would say that we were terribly surprised to see how
quickly it was done. I have the skin of a coyote which
was caught in Cherry County, Nebraska, and if I
wanted to fool anybody by misrepresentations, I
think I could fool nineteen-twentieths or more of all
the people in Central Pennsylvania by showing this
skin and saying it was a genuine Pennsylvania wolf,
but I have no inclination to deceive or fool any one.
The methods of hunting wolves in Pennsylvania are

only a few, as the wolf by nature is a night prowler, and here in this heavy wooded mountainous country the most skillful hunter could not make five cents a day hunting wolves only by hunting for a den where they have their young. The writer only knew of three wolves being shot by hunters while in pursuit of game, unless they were hunting for a wolf den, and then it is not one time in a dozen that the hunter will see one of the old wolves. So you can see the chance of a hunter getting a shot at a wolf is a good way apart and far between. We were acquainted with a good many of the old hunters in four or five Counties and not one in ten of them ever saw a wolf while hunting or trapping, except the wolf was in a trap. Our method of hunting wolves was to train a dog to follow the trail of wolves on bare ground; then in the month of May go into a locality where wolves have been killing sheep. If we could get the trail the first morning after the killing the dog would follow the trail nearly as fast as we cared to walk, but if the trail was a day or two old, we might not be able to keep the trail for 100 rods in a whole day. In a case of this kind we could consult our compass and note the course as nearly as possible, provided these wolves traveled in a straight direction, but if they traveled in any direction to hit every laurel patch or jungle, we dropped that trail quick, for wolves that are rearing young will go as straight to their den after getting a good meal of mutton as a bee will fly to his tree after getting all the

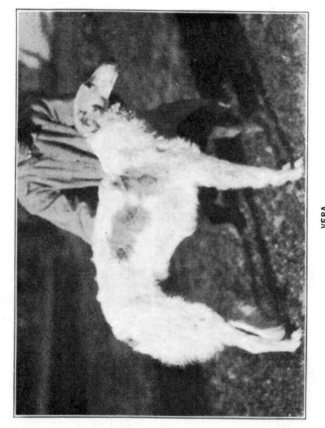

VERA

Pennsylvania-bred, Russian Wolfhound, owned by J. Bailey Wilson, Lansdowne, Pa.

honey he can carry. If you have a good dog and can get a fresh trail of wolves going to their den, you are sure to find the den, but you may not get a wolf after all, for if the den is in a ledge of rocks you may not get a single wolf, for when the young get to be six weeks old they are very cunning and the old ones have been known to leave the locality of their den and not return to that locality for six months or more. And it is seldom they return for three or four weeks. Our method of trapping for them around a den is to set a trap in every path that leads to the den. The most successful method the old time trapper had was path trapping. The best method of trapping for wolves by bait was to throw our bait down in any place in plain sight of some knoll two or three rods away; set a trap on the knoll, for the wolf would go over that knoll a dozen times before he would venture up to the bait. Set no trap nearer the bait than the one on the knoll, but if there should be any old paths near, that is, within fifteen or twenty rods, set a trap in each path. We would not go to these traps oftener than three or four days; then we would go past them just near enough so we could see if they were setting all right; go fifty or a hundred rods and go back on the other side of the valley. Never go to the traps and turn around and go back, for if you do don't expect to catch a wolf in it. We have never made a great fortune hunting or trapping wolves, but we think we have come as near making wages at it as any man in this section during our time, for we have

caught, killed and sold scores of young and old ones
besides what we poisoned. We are certain that we
put quite a number out of commission, possibly a
hundred. Now we hope you won't think hard of us
for using poison on the wolf family. We never used
poison to kill any animals only wolves and rats. All
the wolf dens we ever found were under big rocks
or under a ledge of rocks, but old wolf hunters have
told us they found a nest in a hollow log or in under
a jamb of timber that the wind had blown down, but
the nests or dens we found, most were under big
rocks and one was under a ledge of rocks and the
whelps were so cunning we were not able to coax a
single one out of that nest, and not one of them came
near enough to get into a trap set as far into the hole
as we could reach, and I don't believe the old ones
ever came back to that place that year. This was in
June, 1876. This was the last nest of young wolves
that any one knows of in Northwestern Pennsylvania.
We don't know how many there were in this litter
of whelps, but we know there was a nest of whelps in
there, for they barked at my dog but would not come
out so we could see them, but we are certain they got
into some hole or crevice where they could not get
out. The last wolf I captured and killed was about
May 25th, 1878.

XI. POSSIBLE RE-INTRODUCTION.

FROM the number of hunters who took out licenses in 1913, upwards of two hundred thousand, it would seem that they formed an important part of the population of Pennsylvania. When it is considered how small a return they received for their efforts, their spirit and enthusiasm for the chase seems all the more commendable. Despite the valiant efforts of Dr. Kalbfus there was very little found to kill during the various "open seasons" which came to an end on the first day of 1914. It is to be doubted if five hundred deer were killed in the entire Commonwealth. With such meagre results the time is bound to be at hand when a strong demand will be made to re-stock the forests with game worthy of the name. Civilized men are beginning to find that killing rabbits, quails and squirrels is little better than a barnyard slaughter, that they do not furnish the excitement expected. Intelligent hunters read of struggles with wolves and mountain lions, of coyote coursing, and dispatching grizzlies in the West, and compare it to the feeble pastime of slaying a few mangey rabbits at home, to the disparagement of the home sport. A strong demand will be made to stock the Pennsylvania wilds not with more rabbits, quails, ground-hogs and squirrels, but with savage beasts, such as panthers, brown bears and wolves. Deer and elk are here already, but without the so-called predatory beasts with them, they are sure to deteriorate. Wolf and panther hunting can be made the royal sport of Pennsylvania. Wolves, unmolested except at certain seasons, would soon make themselves at home, and would prove a great benefit alike to sportsmen and to the game animals and birds. As far as damage to sheep is concerned, it would be less than is now done by dogs. As to the best variety of wolf to introduce, the Black Wolf seems to have been able to adjust itself to conditions; it was the last to be exterminated. As far as known the Eastern black wolf is now extinct. The Western timber wolf requires a wider range than Pennsylvania could afford. The grey Pennsylvania wolf is gone, but its congeners in the West Virginia wilds might be introduced with advantage. The brown Pennsylvania wolf is probably extinct, as its relative in North Carolina and Tennessee has been recently killed to the last specimen by professional hunters. The Western coyote might adapt itself, and could be introduced if no other varieties were available. This animal resembles the Pennsylvania brown wolf in many respects. It affords sport wherever it is known, and is hardy, is game and resourceful. The methods of the old Pennsylvania bounty hunters would not be used by the sportsmen of the future. These included trapping, snaring, pitfalls and poisoning. The wolf hunting as practiced in Ireland in the eighteenth century, and in France today would be best suited to present-day needs in the Keystone state. Years ago in England

RAMSDEN REX

English-bred, Russian Wolfhound, owned by Henry W. Shoemaker, McElhattan, Pa.

the open season for hunting wolves was between December 25 and March 25. It furnished ideal "Christmas" sport. A wolf hunt in France is described as follows: "An open spot is generally chosen at some distance from the great coverts where the wolves were known to lie, and here, in concealment, a brace. sometimes two brace, of wolf hounds were placed. A horse was killed and the fore-quarters were trailed through the paths and ways in the wood during the previous day, and back to where the carcass lay, and there they were left. When night approached, out came the wolves, and having struck the scent, they followed it until they found the dead horse, when of course they began to feed on the flesh, and early in the morning, just before day-break, the hunters placed their dogs so as to prevent the wolves from returning to cover. When a wolf came to the spot, the man in charge of the wolf-hounds suffered him to pass by the first, but the last were let slip full in his face, and at the same instant the others were let slip also, the first staying him ever so little, he was sure to be attacked on all sides at once, and therefore, the more easily taken." This is similar to the methods followed by the Grand Dukes at Gatchina in Russia. This aptly portrays the sport of the future for Pennsylvania gentlemen. Could anything be more blood-curdling or inspiring? In Ireland the wealthy gentry hunted wolves on horseback. The animals were baited to come into the open, and then mounted men and wolf-hounds made

after them, the effort being put forth to prevent them
from getting back to cover.   The huntsmen were
armed with spears, and pinioned the fierce beasts to
the earth from their galloping steeds.   In our Western States coyotes, and occasionally timber wolves
are coursed on the open plains by Russian wolf-
hounds, followed by mounted hunters.   The wolves,
if run down, are killed by the pack of dogs or else
shot   by   the   hunters.   This   is   often   done   on
the Russian Steppes, by a stronger race of wolf-
hounds than has been developed as yet in the United
States.   In an effort to arouse interest in a better
type of wolf dogs, the writer offered two special
prizes at the Dog Show of the Westminster Kennel
Club, held in New York in February, 1914, for Russian wolf-hounds which had actually coursed wolves,
or were kept for this purpose in a wolf country.*   At
present the Irish wolf-hound looks to be more capable
of running down wolves than the Russian variety,
which is called the Borzoi.   The breeding and sale
of wolf dogs would add greatly to the incomes of
Pennsylvania mountaineers.   A comparison of the
different varieties of wolf dogs can be gleaned from
the following, which is quoted from the New York
"World:"   "Several years ago General Roger Williams, of Lexington, Ky., was a judge in a wolf hunting contest in Colorado, in which Russian wolf-

---

*One of these prizes was won by Imported Postrel, a
handsome brown dog, a picture of which appears in this
book.

hounds and Scotch deer-hounds contested. Under the stipulations only two dogs could be turned loose on one wolf. Among the Russian dogs was one which had won the gold medals in a wolf-killing contest at St. Petersburg, offered by the Czar, and his owner claimed that he could kill any American wolf. But the Russian dogs failed, so did the Scotch dogs. One of the latter quit fighting for a moment and its owner pulled a revolver and shot the dog dead, saying he would not have a dog which would quit fighting." A letter from California states that Russian wolf-hounds are a failure on ranches where they have been installed for the purpose of killing coyotes and wolves, and do as much damage to live stock as the wolves. The writer of this article is a lover of the Russian wolf-hound, and has bred these dogs since 1906. But he believes the race will have to be strengthened by actual contact with wolves, or it will deteriorate into a mere showy house-pet In 1908 he obtained two coyotes and a European wolf for a chase at McElhattan, Pa. The wolf-hounds did not seem inclined to course the animals, so the chase was never held. The coyotes are now in the Reading Zoo, and the wolf was sold to a traveling showman. According to the newspapers this animal broke out of the wagon and bit a cow which was pasturing peacefully by the road side, and also frightened a little girl. The Russian wolf-hound is a beautiful and intelligent animal, and has been justly called the "aristocrat of the dog kingdom." Perhaps a cross between this breed and the Irish wolf-hound would produce the right sort for Pennsylvania wolf hunting. With all these prospects there is a glorious vista ahead for dog-lovers and true sportsmen, if only we can have our wolves again! We will conclude this chapter by quoting an old Irish poem about a celebrated wolf hunter named McDermot, who was once the terror of the wolves of Munster:

> "It happen'd on a day with horn and hounds,
> A baron gallop't through McDermot's grounds.
> Well hors'd, pursuing o'er the dusty plain
> A wolf that sought the neighboring woods to gain.
> Mac hears th' alarm, and with his oaken spear,
> Joins in the chase, and runs before the peer,
> Outstrips the huntsman, dogs and panting steeds,
> And, struck by him, the falling savage bleeds."

POSTREL

Imported Russian Wolfhound, famed on the steppes of the old country as a Wolf courser

Owned by Hon. Joseph B. Thomas, Middleburg, Virginia

Photo by F. C. Clarke, New York City

XII. SUPERSTITIONS.

LIKE in old world countries, the Pennsylvania wolf gave rise to its share of superstitions. Although only known to residents of the Commonwealth for two centuries, it left an impress that will last for the next five hundred years. Some of the old legends, however, have a tendency to die out with the passing of the aged people, the younger generations evincing little desire to pass them on. There being few open fire-places left to cluster about on cold winter nights, family story telling is fast becoming a lost accomplishment. Furthermore, unimaginative persons object to the hearing or telling of stories the absolute truth of which cannot be vouched for. *Faith* is unthinkable to such practical individuals. Fortunately some few of the older stories are still in existence, and several new ones have cropped up during the past quarter of a century. Of these the most celebrated is the one which the writer of this article related in his volume of legends "Pennsylvania Mountain Stories," in Chapter XIX, called "The Black Wolf of Oak Valley." As the story in question happened within the past twenty years, it was found necessary to alter and disguise names of persons and places. Still there are many who will penetrate this veil and can gather more information upon the subject if interested. It appears that a notorious mountain character, who was wanted by the authorities on several charges, barricaded himself in his log cabin home, resisting arrest. The house was set on fire, but rather than fall into the hands of his enemies the fellow cut his throat and fell back into the flames. Shortly after this a black wolf was noticed running in and out of the oak-wood where he was buried. Hunting parties were organized, but the wolf, despite its boldness, could not be shot. A reputed witch was appealed to, who advised that the outlaw's body be taken from the oak grove and interred in the cemetery of a religious denomination, beside the grave of his mother. This was done and the black wolf was seen no more. Going back a hundred years there is the story of Mrs. Mike McClure, of Wayne Township, Clinton County. This estimable woman had gone to a neighbor's to borrow a Dutch oven. Having secured it, and on her way home she stopped to talk with a friend, Mrs. Jake Simcox, who resided on the bank of the river. She heard a scraping sound by her side, and looking around saw the head of a brown wolf appearing from a pile of rocks. Quick as a flash she seized the Dutch oven, which had on the top an iron circular handle, and bringing it down crushed the wolf's skull. She carried the carcass home, where her husband skinned it, and it was used to cover their infant, which was then in its cradle. So much for that story. Compare it to the following, which is quoted word for word from James E. Hart-

ing's well-known account of the wolves of Scotland.*
"Another story is on record of a wolf killed by a
woman of Cre-Cebhan, near Strui, on the North Side
of the Strath Glass. She had gone to Strui to borrow
a girdle (a thick circular plate of iron, with an iron
loop handle at one side for lifting, and used for bak-
ing bread). Having procured it, and being on her
way home, she sat down upon an old cairn to rest
and gossip with a neighbor, when suddenly a scraping of stones and rustling of dead leaves were heard,
and the head of a wolf protruded from a crevice at
her side. Instead of fleeing in alarm, however, she
dealt him such a blow on the skull with the full swing
of her iron discus, that it brained him on the stone
which served for his emerging head." This empha-
sizes the words of the late Andrew Lang, which were
somewhat like this: "Human nature is very much
the same, despite varying climes and creeds." This
story is probably centuries old, and similar occur-
rences have revived its details in the minds of the
old people. Another "were-wolf" of Central Pennsylvania also had its *habitat* in Wayne Township.
George Wilson long suspected that a certain woman
in his neighborhood was a witch, and went about in
wolfish form at nightfall. One evening at dusk he
saw the wolf, which was of extraordinary size, and
brown in color, crossing a field back of his cabin. He
quickly loaded his rifle with a silver bullet, and made
after the intruder. Taking careful aim he fired, but

*In "Extinct British Animals."

the darkness was too far advanced to make his aim accurate, although he was a famous marksman. He struck the animal in the left fore-leg, and it disappeared into the forest at the foot of the (lower) Bald Eagle Mountain, howling piteously. He had barely gotten into his house when the supposed witch rushed into the cabin of a settler, who lived about a mile away, with her left arm broken just above the wrist. The arm was put in splints, but it never became straight again. It is interesting to note that in the Seven Mountains the ghost wolves were always black, in the West Branch Valley brown, and in the Northern part of the state grey, showing the influence of the prevailing type on the imagination. The old people in the Seven Mountains declared that the Black Wolf's bark said plainly: "Dead Indian, Dead Indian, where, where, where!"

GREY WOLF

Killed by Bud Dalrymple, Scenic, S. D., January 9, 1914

This specimen, which was pure white, was very old

XIII. BRAVEST OF THE BRAVE.

THAT the presence of wolves in a country brings out the bravest characteristics in mankind cannot be denied. It is the *pabulum* of heroes. Some families have fought wolves for generations, and in the wars of men they demonstrate what they have learned of valor in the chase. Take the Quinn family, for instance. Their crest is a wolf's head, *erased,* argent. They have been known as a race of wolf hunters and warriors in the North of Ireland for centuries. Terence Quinn was known among the earliest Indian fighters in Central Pennsylvania, and escaped from the awful massacre at Dry Valley in 1778. He was a noted wolf hunter in his day. His son, Samuel Michael Quinn, was appointed an ensign in the rangers commanded by the celebrated Peter Grove. In 1788 young Quinn, then in his twentieth year, was selected as an assistant surveyor and sent into the wild regions of the West Branch. He camped at the mouth of the run which was named after him, Quinn's Run, near the present town of Lock Haven. Modern innovators have changed the name of the run to Queen's Run. One of the young surveyor's companions, Peter Farley by name, was seized with an attack of pneumonia, and confined to his bunk in the shack, which stood on the bank of the run where it emptied into the Susquehanna. A panther's tracks were noticed in the snow, and young Quinn went after it, accompanied by his faithful bull dogs. After a long chase he overtook it at the head of Rattlesnake Run, where the Blanchard cabin was afterwards built. Far up in an enormous white pine, the stab of which is still standing, the panther was crouched, its bright eyes, to use the hunter's own words, "glowed like the eyes of a demon." Quietly and quickly he raised his gun and fired, then stepped back and began to re-load his muzzle-loader. As he did so the mammoth brute came tumbling down, its dead body falling in the big spring. Carrying the handsome hide, the hunter returned towards his cabin, thinking to cheer his sick companion with the story of his exploit. As he neared the shack the bull dogs began showing signs of alarm. It was almost dark, but he could make out four wolves crouched close together outside the door, motionless, their long noses scenting the warm air which came from beneath the door. His gun being re-loaded with a heavy bullet, he took careful aim and fired, before the wolves could become aware of his proximity. The heavy charge penetrated the throats of all four wolves, killing them instantly. The shot aroused the sick man and he called out, "Is that you, Mickey," to which the young hunter replied in cheery affirmative. He pushed open the door, kicking the carcasses of the four wolves before him. Peter Farley, who lived to be nearly ninety, said that he could never forget the sight which greeted his eyes. In the doorway stood Quinn with the panther hide over his shoulder, and the four dead wolves piled up about his feet. The dogs formed the background of the picture. The excitement was a help to the sick man, and he soon recovered. The two young men killed, while camped at Quinn's Run, over one hundred wolves, which naturally reduced the boldness of these animals in that neighborhood. Later in life Samuel Quinn returned to Buffalo Valley, where he became a noted patron of sport. He loved good horses, and encouraged horse racing in that region. On his way down country he found a stray horse in a forest. On its back were remnants of a saddle, showing that it had once belonged to some trader who had been ambushed and slain by redmen. The young ranger was fleet of foot, and ran after it, and caught it by the mane. The animal was a dark brown in color, with a white face, well put together and was an entire. Quinn made a rude bridle out of hides and rode the animal home.* On the way a pack of wolves put in an appearance, and the young nimrod shot a dozen of them from the horse's back, in the true old-fashioned Irish style. He used the brown horse for many years as a stock horse, and the dam of Sea Turtle, which won a twelve mile race from the Great Island to Jersey Shore, about 1835, was one of his numerous progeny.

---

*He called it AOIDH, which is the Gaelic for STRANGER.

XIV. CATCHING WOLVES WITH FISH HOOKS.

M R. C. W. DICKINSON is very fond of relating the following remarkable anecdote, which he has written out, and which is reproduced verbatim:

I will try to give you an account of a hunting and fishing trip when we caught two wolves with a fish-hook. On May 14th, 1872, the writer started out to find a den or nest of young wolves. As there had been numerous losses of sheep slaughtered by wolves over a territory of about fifteen miles square, we had learned by experience that somewhere within this territory there was a den of wolves consisting of two old wolves and a litter of whelps. On this point we were dead certain. But in what locality was this den? From experience we had learned that these cunning brutes would not kill sheep at this season of the year within three or four miles of their den, and as three-fourths of this territory was a solid forest and the den might be outside of this territory, as wolves have been known to go fifteen or twenty miles from their den to kill sheep when they were rearing their young. In the Southwestern part of this territory and a mile and a half from any neighbors lived an old German by the name of Adam Martin who kept quite a flock of sheep, wintering annually from 60 to 100 shee~ His farm was on top of the mountain, and the East

GREY WOLF
Caught by front foot and lower jaw in steel traps
From Fur News Magazine

Photo by A. B. Wolf, of Colorado

side of his farm joined an abandoned farm of three hundred acres of cleared land, which Mr. Martin utilized as a pasture for all his stock, except his hogs and calves, which he kept near his house so it would be handy to feed them. Mr. Martin's sheep ran at will on the abandoned farm from the time snow went off in the Spring until he drove them to his barn after winter set in. During four years prior to May 14th he did not lose a single sheep by wolves. We looked at this fact as being almost positive proof that the wolf den was within two or three miles of this abandoned farm, which is located on top of the mountain between Red Mill Brook and Robin's Brook. These two streams empty into Potato Creek about four miles East of the abandoned farm. So on May 14th we set out in quest of the wolf den with our knapsack on our back, containing three wolf traps, a small quantity of salt and three or four days' rations for myself and my faithful dog Rover, which always was my companion on my hunting or trapping expeditions while he lived. During Spring, Summer and Fall a hunter or trapper always carried a fish line, a few extra hooks and package of salt. In case provisions began to run low he could catch all the trout in fifteen minutes a man could eat at one meal. After traveling about eight miles we came on the old abandoned farm known as the Bunker Hill farm. We took to the tall timber in a Northwesterly direction In less than an hour we had the trail of wolves, which Rover could follow about as fast as I cared to walk.

After we followed this trail for twenty minutes we left it, as the wolves seemed to be going in all directions, just looking for a woodchuck, coon or a rabbit to make a meal of. We started on our original course and in about thirty minutes we had another trail which was zig-zagging around as bad as a fox in a meadow hunting mice. These crooked trails we did not want. We wanted to find the trail of wolves that were traveling in a straight line in any one direction, for that was the trail to lead us to the den, so we struck out again. About 2.30 P. M. we struck a trail that looked better to me, as they were traveling a little East of South and going as straight as a bee would fly to his tree. We followed this trail until after sundown, came to a small spring run and decided to camp for the night by this run so as to have water handy for supper and breakfast. We gathered a pile of old chunks of wood for a fire, for at this season of the year the nights are cold in the mountains. After we got a good camp fire started we ate our supper and we began to howl like a wolf and kept this up at intervals of every twenty minutes until 10.30, when we got two wolves to answer us. They were on top of the mountain and Northeast of us. In about forty minutes they answered us again on the top of a hill to the Northwest and about a half mile away. Next time they answered South of us and clear at the top of the mountain. We knew they were about in the edge of the Northeast corner of Bunker Hill farm. Then we laid down by the camp fire and went to sleep. We were up with the birds in the morning, ate our breakfast and ready to start on the trail just as the sun came in sight in the East. Right here we made a blunder as the dog wanted to take the trail we were following the night before, while I had made up my mind to go to the top of the mountain where the wolves had answered me first the evening before. When we went about one-third the distance to the hill top we found a path or trail that only an experienced woodsman would detect. This path led straight up or down the hill and as old Rover wanted to go down hill we decided to follow him. We had gone about thirty rods when we came to a flat rock. This rock was about level on top and about sixteen feet square. The ground on the hill side was as high as the rock, while the down hill side of the rock was about three feet above the ground. The leaves that had fallen from the trees for ages lay on this rock the same as they did on the ground around it. Here on top of this rock, about the center part of it, was something that looked nice to me. Here in the leaves was a wolf's bed that had been occupied many times. It resembled a dog's bed in a straw pile; a ring of leaves about six inches high, all worn fine. And at this season of the year, being the time all animals shed their winter coat, there was wolf hair enough in this bed, and mixed with the broken leaves in the ring around it to make a dozen bird's nests. Now, we were sure we were going to find the coveted prize. As we looked for the path from this rock we could not see any, so decided we were "in wrong" and retraced our path up the hill. After we had gone six or eight rods past the point where we first hit this path, we noticed a path coming into the path we were following, but at the angle the path came would indicate we were going in the wrong direction. A few rods farther on a path came in on the opposite side and a little further on another path, and other paths, and auguring wrong for us to be going in the right direction, and the path we were following kept getting smaller until we got on top of the mountain, when we did not have any path. As it was very cold, there being a heavy frost, and the sun shone in through an open space, we sat on an old log in the sunlight to get warm and to think the subject over. After a few minutes we thought we would howl and see if the wolves would answer us. In about two seconds one of them answered. It was about fifty rods away in an easterly direction. Before the sound had died away the other one answered about the same distance away, but to the West. They kept howling to each other so we kept still and waited. The sound of the one East was getting nearer. Directly we saw the animal coming. We got in position to shoot it, but to our surprise our rifle would not stand cocked. We tried to hold the hammer back with our thumb and shoot by letting the hammer slip from under the thumb, but the thumb hid the sights so the wolf got away with a whole hide. I took out my pocket knife, used a blade for a screw

PAIR OF YOUNG COYOTES

From Fur News Magazine

driver, took the lock off and found that oil that had been put on the lock the Fall before had become gummy and thick and the cold night had made it so hard it would not let the "dog" work enough to catch in the cocked notch. After scraping the thick oil out with the point of a knife blade I found the lock would work all right. After putting the lock back in place we retraced our steps back down hill to the flat rock wondering all the time at what made the path end so abruptly at that point. Two or three years prior to this a beech tree that stood at the upper edge of the rock had broken off and fallen down the hill over this rock. The force of this tree falling down hill had carried the butt of the tree about half way across the rock. As we got to this rock old Rover trotted through the bed, jumped on to the butt of the tree, trotted down the log until he got among the limbs, jumped off on the right side, and as soon as he started from the log I could see the path very plain. I stopped him, went down to where he was, told him to go on; he went about five rods to the side of a large rock that was about fifteen feet high and about thirty feet square. The dog walked along to the corner of the rock, turned to the right, and as soon as I turned this corner the dog was looking into a large hole under and about the middle of the rock. The first glance told us we had the den sure, whether we got any wolves or not. We let the dog go in under the rock and after a minute called him out by chirping to him. The young wolves followed him to the mouth of the hole. There were seven of them, pretty little "cusses" too, but how were we to get them? That was the perplexing problem. We began to look for a small sapling that forked out three or four feet from the ground. We soon found one, the prong being about six feet long. These prongs we twisted into switches, taking hold of the two switched prongs about half way to the top from the point where they separated from the prongs together with the tops of each prong pointing in opposite directions, then tied them with a small string, then wound the top end of one prong around the butt end of the other several times to the point they pronged, tied this fast then wound the other side in the same way. This left a hoop about two feet in diameter. We took our hatchet, cut the sapling so the part below the prongs was three feet long. This we used as a handle to manipulate the withe hoop. We sent the dog into the den. As soon as we heard the whelps whining around the dog we chirped to him. He came out, the whelps trotting along with him until they were within two feet of the hole. We had one hoop in position before calling the dog out. We stood as much out of sight as possible and allow us to see into the hole, holding our hoop close up against the rock and when the little "brats" stopped to bark at us we dropped the hoop over two of them, giving them a quick jerk. They rolled out doors about three feet. We dropped our hoop and clinched them. Holy smoke, how they did yell. At first they tried to bite, but as soon as they found out we were not going to hurt them we could handle them as well as you could handle little puppies. four or five weeks old. The experience we had with other dens in former years, we were certain we could not fool these little chaps again the same day. We went forty rods from the den, cut three clogs, one for each trap we had with us; we set a trap in the two paths that seemed to be the most traveled. Then we went back, let the dog go under the rock again, but nothing doing. Could not get a whine from the little fellows. We went and cut a little sapling a little larger, for a good fish pole, cut the top off at a point where the pole was three-eighth of an inch in diameter, tied the largest fish-hook we had on to the top end of the pole. Then we crawled under the rock as far as the cavity was large enough for us to go, then ran the pole on under the rock, judging from the feeling to tell whether it hit a stone or hard ground or an animal. Directly I was sure it hit an animal. I gave a little jerk and at that a young wolf began to "ki-yi." I backed out from under the rock pulling the pole with me, and I pulled the little wolf out. We found the hook was fast in the muscles of his foreleg close to the body. After getting the hook out of the leg we put the pup into the knapsack and crawled into the den again, and in less than five minutes we had another one hooked. This one was hooked through the left forefoot. After getting him off the hook we crawled under again and fished until we were so tired we had to quit, and as it was late in the afternoon we set the remaining trap in the hole and went home taking the four wolves with us. Early the next morning we took six wolf traps and went back to the den. On arriving there we found everything as we had left it the day before. We took up the trap in the hole as cautious as possible, got my hoop and let the dog go under. We soon heard the whelps whining. We chirped to the dog and as he came out one whelp came close enough. We caught him with the hoop. Then we tried the fish pole again. Nothing doing! We went and set the six traps in the paths that came in towards the den. We went to the den, let the dog go under again, but nothing doing. Tried the fish pole again. Got nothing. We had a heavy chalk line with us. I took the wolf we got in the morning, tied this chalk line to his neck, crawled under as far as I could get and let him go back into the den, letting the line out as fast as he went in. He went whining along until he found company. Then we began to pull him back. He began to whine and kept it up until we drew him up to us. Now it was as dark as night, our body filled the hole so we could see nothing. We felt back of the one we had and got one of the remaining ones by a leg hold on to him, backed out of the den; so now we had six out of the seven. A cousin of mine, a slim, puny boy of sixteen, wanted to go with me this day and I took him along as he was so anxious to see a wolf den, and as it was afternoon we went to where I had camped the first night out, to eat our dinner. It was not over

THE ANTIQUARIAN

From a photo by Mrs. Henry W. Shoemaker

fifty rods from the den. After dinner I asked my
cousin to go trout fishing with me for an hour or
two. He said he would rather lie down and sleep,
as he got up so early, so I went fishing for one and
a half hours and caught 85 nice trout, but on my return I was startled not to find the boy. I hollowed
as loud as I could yell, but got no answer. As we
looked around we noticed our knapsack was gone and
the two wolves with it. The thought struck us the
boy might have gone to the den, so we ran to it and
got there just in time to see that boy back out from
under the rock with the seventh wolf. Now, we don't
believe that there was another boy of his size and age
within the State that could have been hired to go
there into that den. We kept our traps set in the
paths for two months and did not catch a thing except hedgehogs, rabbits and woodchucks.

XV.   HISTORICAL EVIDENCE.

BEFORE bringing to a close this treatise on the wolves of Pennsylvania it might be well to mention some evidences of their historical antiquity and connection with the early Indians. After the Erie Indians had been vanquished and departed from the region South of Lake Erie it was not occupied by any Indians for a number of years. As a consequence the entire country south of the Lake became infested with great packs of wolves. When the distinguished explorer Rene La Salle passed along the Southern shore of Lake Erie in 1680, the wolves had increased to such numbers as to endanger travel through the entire region. The present Crawford, Mercer and other Northwestern Counties were swarming with wolves when the first travelers passed through that region. Wolf Creek (or Tummeink, "Place of Wolves"), in Mercer and Butler Counties, is a name which no doubt belongs to this period of wolves. The early French pioneers called the Lenni-Lenape Indians "Wolves," because they were first brought into contact with the Munsee, the "Wolf" tribe of the Lenni-Lenape. The name of this clan was "Took-seat," meaning "Round Paw," and having reference to the wolf. The Minsi (often confused with the Munsee) was the "Wolf" clan of the Munsee tribe. A Minsi or Minisink, was a member of the wolf clan of the Wolf tribe of the Lenni-Lenape. During the various periods of Indian hostilities in what is now Pennsylvania the Munsee, and especially the Minsi, were the most hostile to the white settlers because of having been driven from the country adjacent to the Delaware River by the various purchases of the Penn family, and then driven from the Susquehanna, notably at Wyoming, by the various Susquehanna purchases. The Munsee were usually allied with the Mchickons and the Senecas and became veritable "wolves" in their raids on settlements. The above information was furnished to the writer by Rev. George P. Donehoo, of Coudersport, Pa., one of the great authorities on the Indian period in Pennsylvania and recently elected secretary of the Historical Commission. The history of the Indians is closely interwoven with that of the wolves, and further researches will surely unearth a wealth of interesting materials.

FINIS.

Metalmark Books is a joint imprint of The Pennsylvania State University
Press and the Office of Digital Scholarly Publishing at The Pennsylvania State
University Libraries. The facsimile editions published under this
imprint are reproductions of out-of-print, public domain works that hold
a significant place in Pennsylvania's rich literary and cultural past.
Metalmark editions are primarily reproduced from the University Libraries' extensive
Pennsylvania collections and in cooperation with other
state libraries. These volumes are available to the public for viewing online
and can be ordered as print-on-demand paperbacks.

LIBRARY OF CONGRESS CATALOGING-IN-PUBLICATION DATA

Shoemaker, Henry W., 1880–1958, author.
Wolf days in Pennsylvania / by Henry W. Shoemaker.
pages   cm
Summary: "A collection of stories about wolves in Pennsylvania, originally published in 1914. Includes interviews with some of the state's famous wolf hunters
and period photographs of the hunters and their prey"—Provided by publisher.
ISBN 978-0-271-06698-1 (pbk. : alk. paper)
1. Wolves—Pennsylvania.
2. Wolf hunting—Pennsylvania.
I. Title.

QL737.C22S538 2015
599.773—dc23
2015008617

Printed in the United States of America
Reprinted by The Pennsylvania State University Press, 2015
University Park, PA 16802-1003

Printed in the United States
By Bookmasters